Deep Space Discovery

The Milky Way and Other Galaxies

GAIL TERP

BLACK RABBIT BOOKS

Bolt is published by Black Rabbit Books
P.O. Box 3263, Mankato, Minnesota, 56002.
www.blackrabbitbooks.com

Marysa Storm, editor; Grant Gould, designer;
Omay Ayres, photo researcher

Library of Congress Cataloging-in-Publication Data
Names: Terp, Gail, 1951- author.
Title: The Milky Way and other galaxies / by Gail Terp.
Description: Mankato, Minnesota : Black Rabbit Books, [2019] | Series: Bolt. Deep space discovery | Audience: Ages 9-12. | Audience: Grades 4 to 6. | Includes bibliographical references and index.
Identifiers: LCCN 2017019662 (print) | LCCN 2017028456 (ebook) | ISBN 9781680725360 (ebook) | ISBN 9781680724202 (library binding) | ISBN 9781680727142 (paperback)
Subjects: LCSH: Galaxies–Juvenile literature. | Milky Way–Juvenile literature. | Universe–Juvenile literature.
Classification: LCC QB857.3 (ebook) | LCC QB857.3 .T47 2019 (print) | DDC 523.1/12-dc23
LC record available at https://lccn.loc.gov/2017019662

Printed in China. 3/18

Image Credits

apod.nasa.gov: NASA, 12–13, 26 (bttm); en.wikipedia.org: NASA/ESA, 27; Nick Risinger, Cover (bkgd); hubblesite.org: NASA, cover (telescope); jwst.nasa.gov: NASA/JWST, 28–29; nasa.gov: NASA, 9, 16–17, 25; photojournal.jpl.nasa.gov: NASA, 22; Science Source: David A. Hardy, 26 (top); Mark Garlick, 15; Shutterstock: Alex Mit, 29; Bupu, 3; Denis Belitsky, 4–5; Merydolla, 18–19, 32; Natykach Nataliia, 31; NikoNomad, 1; Triff, 6; vectortatu, 10–11; Vladi333, 21

CONTENTS

CHAPTER 1

The MILKY WAY

A white band stretches far across the night sky. It glimmers and sparkles. It seems to go on forever. Long ago, people looked up at this band. They thought it looked like spilled milk. They called it the Milky Way.

Planets are large bodies that orbit stars. Earth and seven other planets circle the sun. They are part of the solar system.

Reach for the Stars

The Milky Way is a galaxy. Earth's solar system is a tiny part of it.

People dream of exploring the Milky Way. But for now, a trip across it isn't possible. It's far too big. Crossing the Milky Way would take about 2 billion years.

CHAPTER 2

What Is a GALAXY?

Galaxies are huge collections of stars and their planets. Some galaxies have trillions of stars.

Dust and gas are also in galaxies. When stars die, they leave behind dust and gas. New stars form from that dust and gas.

Some scientists believe there are up to 2 trillion galaxies.

TYPES OF GALAXIES

There are three basic kinds of galaxies.

long arms

spiral

pinwheel-shaped

stars mostly form in the arms

made up of mostly old stars

elliptical

oval-shaped

made up of mostly
young stars

irregular

uneven shape

On the Move

Galaxies do not stay in one spot. They travel through space. When galaxies get near each other, they often combine.

Galaxies are huge. So when they combine, stars rarely hit each other. They stay too far apart. The joining can take millions of years.

CHAPTER 3

A CLOSER LOOK at the Milky Way

The Milky Way is a barred spiral galaxy. It's shaped like a thin disk. A bar of stars extends from its center. In the middle of the Milky Way is a **bulge**. It is made up of stars, gas, and dust. From it, arms of stars and dust swirl out. There are 100 to 400 billion stars in the Milky Way. Gas and old stars surround the galaxy.

Barred Spiral Galaxies

About
50 to 70%
of spiral galaxies
are barred.

Scientists believe a black hole forms when a large star dies.

Black Hole

A black hole is at the Milky Way's center. Despite its name, a black hole isn't a hole. It's a place with incredibly strong **gravity**. Gravity's pull is so strong nothing can escape it. Black holes take in dust and gas. They pull stars apart.

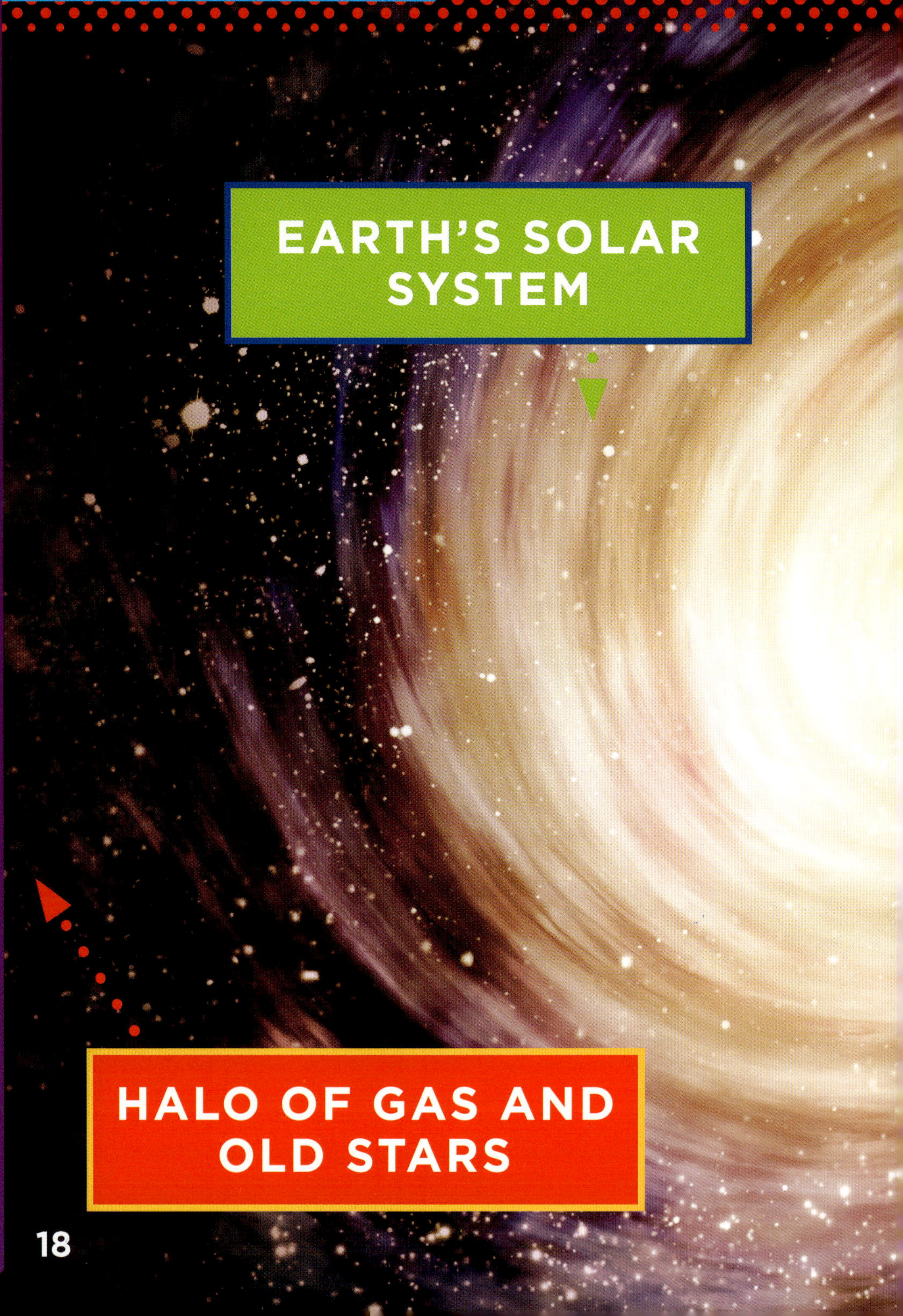
EARTH'S SOLAR SYSTEM
HALO OF GAS AND OLD STARS

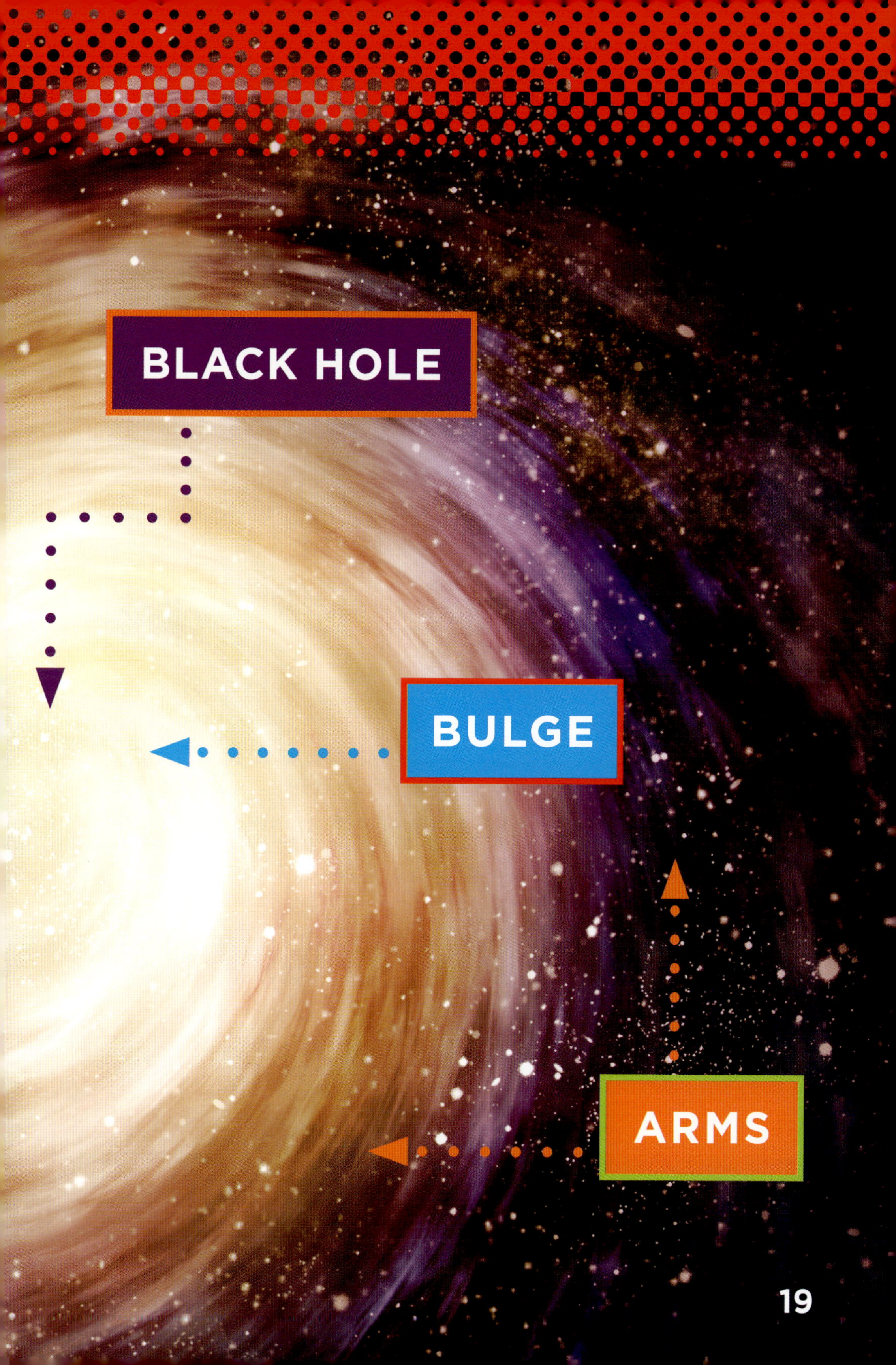
BLACK HOLE
BULGE
ARMS

CHAPTER 4

BEYOND the Milky Way

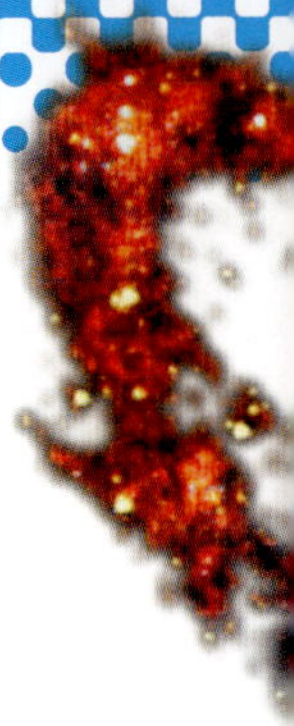

Space is full of giant galaxies. Andromeda (also called M31) is the closest to the Milky Way. It is 2.5 million light-years away. In time, it will **collide** with the Milky Way. But people don't need to worry. M31 won't arrive for billions of years.

light-year

A light-year measures distance. It's how far light travels in one year. One light-year is about 5.9 trillion miles (9.5 trillion kilometers).

The Triangulum Galaxy (M33)

Like the Milky Way, M33 is a spiral galaxy. It is 3 million light-years from the Milky Way. M33 is full of gas clouds. Scientists call these clouds **stellar** nurseries. Many large stars form inside them.

Large stars don't live as long as small stars.

The Pinwheel Galaxy (M101)

Galaxies can be beautiful to look at. And M101 is no exception. Its swirls of stars and dust are well-defined. It is about 70 percent larger than the Milky Way.

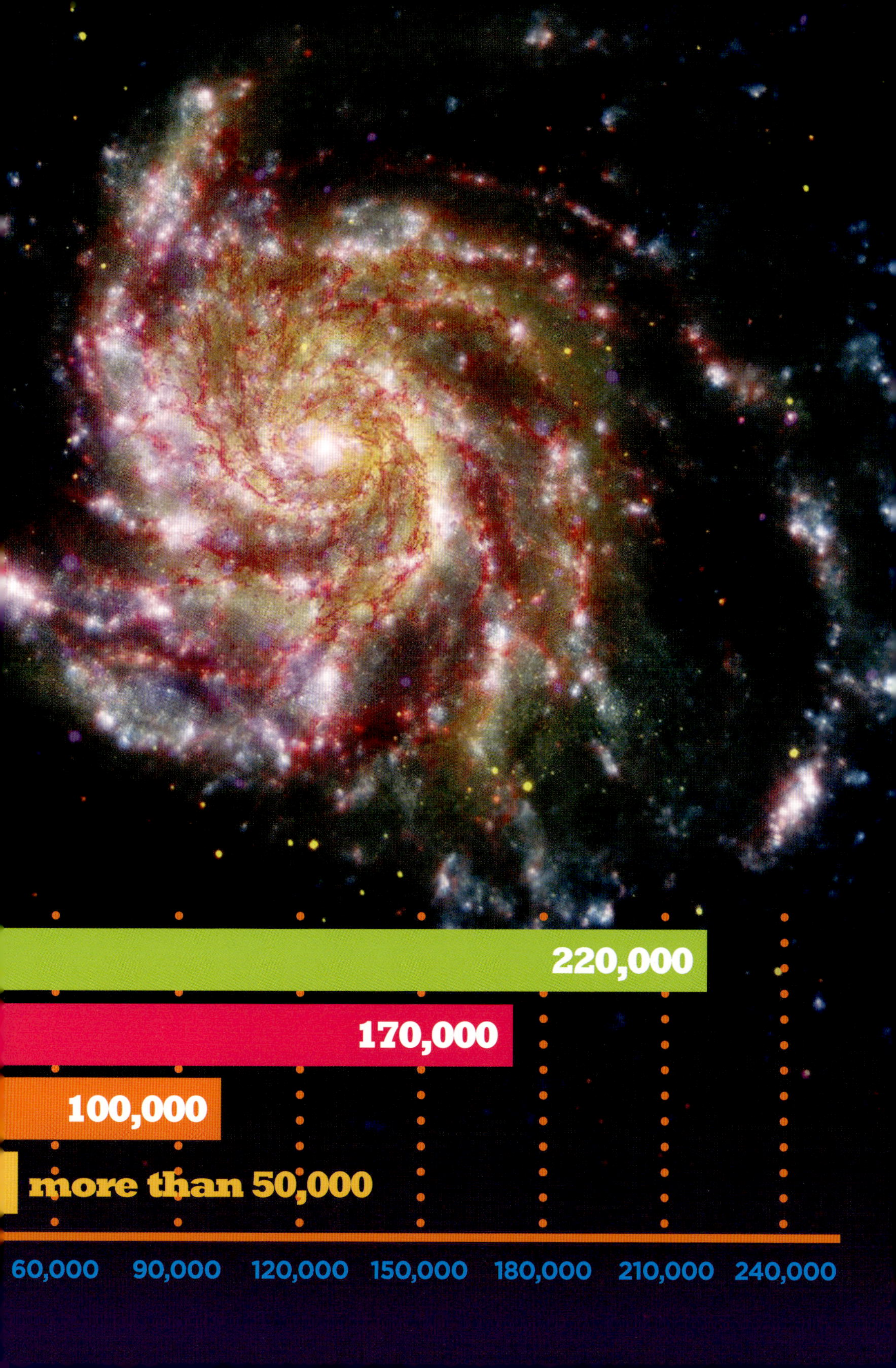
220,000
170,000
100,000
more than 50,000
60,000
90,000
120,000
150,000
180,000
210,000
240,000

Part of Something Bigger

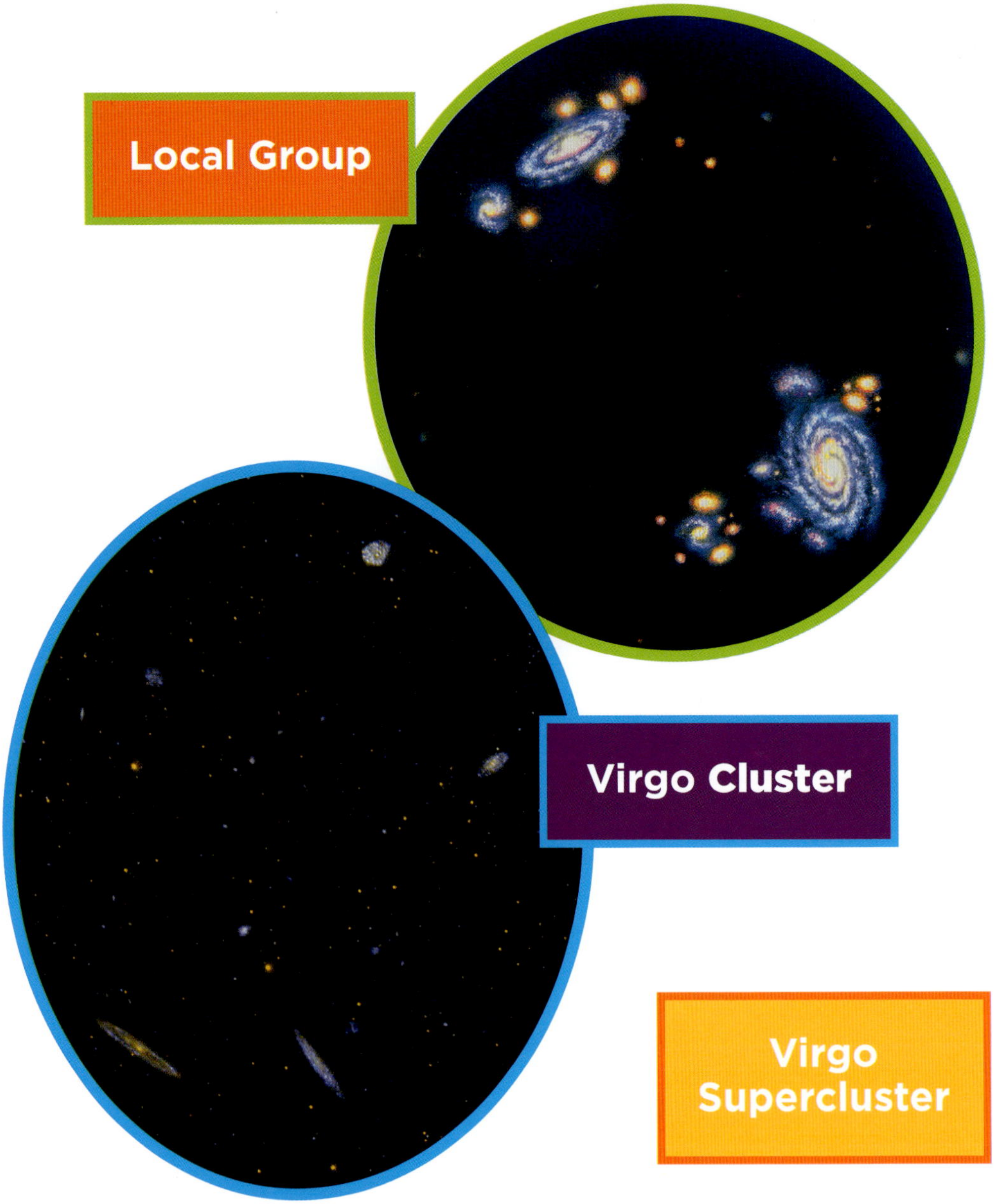

The Local Group

Galaxies form clusters. Thousands of galaxies can exist in just one cluster. Clusters form groups. They are called superclusters.

The Milky Way, M31, and M33 belong to one group. It is called the Local Group. The group is part of the Virgo Cluster. And that cluster is part of the Virgo Supercluster. Scientists believe this supercluster is home to 1 million galaxies.

Learning More

People have studied galaxies for hundreds of years. But there is still much to learn. New technology will make that possible. Better telescopes and spacecraft will show galaxies in more detail. New discoveries will teach people more about the Milky Way. People will learn more about the **universe** they call home.

bulge (BUHLJ)—a part that sticks out

cluster (KLUHS-ter)—a group of things that are close together

collide (kuh-LAHYD)—to hit something or each other with strong force

elliptical (ih-LIP-ti-kuhl)—to have an oval shape

gravity (GRAV-i-tee)—the natural force that pulls physical things toward each other

orbit (AWR-bit)—the path taken by one body circling around another body

stellar (STEL-er)—made up of stars

universe (YOO-nuh-vurs)—all of space and everything in it

LEARN MORE

BOOKS

Hudak, Heather C. *Galaxies.* Exploring Our Universe. Minneapolis: Abdo Pub., 2017.

Riggs, Kate. *Galaxies.* Across the Universe. Mankato, MN: Creative Education/Creative Paperbacks, 2015.

Roland, James. *Black Holes: A Space Discovery Guide.* Space Discovery Guides. Minneapolis: Lerner Publications, 2017.

WEBSITES

Black Hole Rescue!
spaceplace.nasa.gov/black-hole-rescue/en/

Milky Way Galaxy
kids.nationalgeographic.com/explore/space/milky-way/#milky-way-2.jpg

Stars and Galaxies
www.esa.int/esaKIDSen/SEM536WJD1E_OurUniverse_0.html

INDEX